EXPLORING INDIA'S CULTURE AND TRADITION

TUSHAR RAJ

Dear Reader,

I am thrilled to present "Exploring India's Culture and Tradition" to you, a comprehensive guide that delves deep into the fascinating and diverse heritage of this incredible country.

This book is dedicated to all those who want to gain a deeper understanding of India's rich cultural tapestry and the traditions that make it unique. It is my hope that this book will provide you with a rich and meaningful experience, whether you are a first-time visitor or a seasoned traveler to India.

I would like to express my gratitude to the countless individuals who have helped to shape and preserve India's culture and traditions over the centuries. From the ancient sages who recorded the Vedas and Upanishads to the modern-day artists and artisans who continue to create masterpieces of art, music, and dance, India's culture is a testament to the human spirit's enduring creativity and resilience.

Finally, I would like to extend my heartfelt appreciation to my family, friends, and colleagues, who have supported me throughout this journey. Without their encouragement, this book would not have been possible.

Thank you for joining me on this exploration of India's culture and tradition. I hope you enjoy the journey as much as I have.

Warm regards,

Tushar Raj

Contents

Foreword

Dear Reader,

Welcome to "Exploring India's Culture and Tradition." In this book, we embark on a journey to unravel the richness and diversity of India's culture and tradition, which has captivated people around the world for centuries.

India is a land of many colors, languages, religions, and beliefs. Its history spans thousands of years, and each era has left an indelible mark on its culture, traditions, and people. From the ancient Indus Valley Civilization to the Mughal Empire, British Raj, and modern-day India, every phase of India's history has contributed to its vibrant cultural tapestry.

This book is a window into the many facets of Indian culture and tradition. We will explore its art, music, dance, literature, cuisine, festivals, and religious practices. We will also delve into the country's diversity, language, and beliefs. Through this exploration, you will discover how Indian culture and tradition have evolved and flourished over time and continue to thrive today.

India's culture and tradition are not only fascinating but also important to understand. They offer us a glimpse into the country's past, present, and future. They connect us to the people, places, and customs of India, and they inspire us to learn, appreciate, and celebrate the world's diversity.

We hope this book will spark your curiosity, deepen your understanding, and enrich your appreciation of India's culture and tradition. We invite you to join us on this exciting journey of exploration.

Happy reading!

Sincerely,

Tushar Raj

Preface

Namaste!

Welcome to "Exploring India's Culture and Tradition," a fascinating journey into the diverse and colorful world of India.

India is a country that has a rich and vibrant history, which is reflected in its culture and tradition. It is a land of myriad cultures, languages, and religions, all coming together to form a beautiful tapestry that is uniquely Indian. From bustling cities to the quiet countryside, India is a country that has something for everyone.

This book is for anyone who is curious about India, its people, and its culture. It is a collection of stories, facts, and insights that will take you on a journey through the various aspects of Indian culture and tradition. You will learn about the vibrant festivals, delicious cuisine, exquisite handicrafts, and breathtaking art forms that are an integral part of India's cultural heritage.

In this book, we have made an effort to showcase the diversity and richness of Indian culture, and we hope that it will inspire you to explore this fascinating country further. Whether you are a seasoned traveler, a student, or simply someone who is curious about the world around you, we hope that this book will provide you with a glimpse into the unique and beautiful culture of India.

We would like to express our gratitude to the people of India, who have been the inspiration behind this book. We hope that this book will serve as a tribute to the rich cultural heritage of India and that it will help to promote greater understanding and appreciation of this beautiful country and its people.

Enjoy the journey!

Acknowledgements

Dear Readers,

We would like to take a moment to express our gratitude to all the people who have contributed to the making of this book, "Exploring India's Culture and Tradition". This book would not have been possible without the help and support of many individuals and organizations, and we would like to extend our heartfelt thanks to each and every one of them.

Firstly, we would like to thank the people of India for their warm hospitality and generosity. We have been fortunate enough to meet and learn from many Indians who have shared their knowledge, stories, and experiences with us. We are grateful for their willingness to open up and let us into their lives, homes, and communities. It is through their guidance and insights that we have been able to gain a deeper understanding and appreciation of India's culture and traditions.

We would also like to acknowledge the various organizations and institutions that have supported us in our research and writing. We extend our thanks to the libraries, museums, archives, and cultural centers that have provided us with access to their collections, resources, and expertise. We would also like to thank the scholars, experts, and practitioners who have generously shared their knowledge and insights with us, and who have helped us to navigate the complexities and nuances of India's culture and traditions.

Furthermore, we would like to thank our families, friends, and colleagues for their encouragement, support, and patience throughout the process of writing this book. We are grateful for their understanding and tolerance of our long hours, late nights, and occasional absences. Their love and support have sustained us through the ups and downs of this project.

Lastly, we would like to express our gratitude to our publisher and editorial team for their guidance, feedback, and support. We appreciate their professionalism, expertise, and enthusiasm, and we are proud to have worked with such a dedicated and talented team.

Once again, we would like to thank everyone who has contributed to the making of this book. It is truly a collective effort, and we are grateful for the support and generosity that we have received along the way.

Sincerely,

Tushar Raj

Prologue

Welcome to "Exploring India's Culture and Tradition"!

India is a land of diversity and rich heritage that has fascinated people for centuries. The country's cultural and traditional roots run deep and are as varied as the languages spoken and the regions that make up this fascinating land. India is a country that boasts a long and complex history, and its culture reflects the country's journey through time.

In this book, we will delve deep into India's vibrant culture and tradition, from its colorful festivals and religious practices to its mouth-watering cuisine and ancient art forms. We will explore the diverse customs and rituals of the country's many regions, from the north to the south, the east to the west, and everything in between.

We'll take a closer look at the daily lives of the people of India, their customs, and the values that are at the heart of their society. We'll examine the importance of family and community, the art of hospitality, and the deep reverence for nature that permeates Indian culture.

In addition, we will explore the fascinating history and architecture of India's magnificent palaces, forts, and temples, and the art and craft of the country's many regions.

Whether you are planning a visit to India, are an admirer of its culture, or are simply interested in learning about this fascinating country, this book is the perfect guide to help you uncover the richness of India's culture and tradition. So, come with us on this incredible journey, and let's explore the wonders of India together!

Author Info

Tushar Raj

@tusharraj9090

ONE

India's Cultural Diversity

India is a country of diverse cultures and traditions. From the snow-capped mountains of the Himalayas to the tropical beaches of the south, India is home to a rich tapestry of people, languages, religions, customs, and traditions. Its cultural diversity is a result of centuries of migration, invasions, and the influence of various religions and belief systems.

India has 28 states, each with its own distinct culture and traditions. For example, in the state of Punjab, the Bhangra dance is a famous tradition, while in the state of Kerala, the Kathakali dance is popular. In the state of Gujarat, people celebrate Navratri with Garba, while in West Bengal, the Durga Puja festival is celebrated with great enthusiasm.

India's cultural diversity is also shaped by the various religions that are practiced in the country. Hinduism is the dominant religion in India, and many cultural traditions are influenced by its practices. However, India is also home to other major religions such as Islam, Christianity, Buddhism, Jainism, and Sikhism, which all have their unique customs and traditions.

Apart from religious and regional differences, India's cultural diversity is also reflected in its food, clothing, and art. Indian cuisine is famous for its use of spices and flavors, and every region has its own unique dishes and styles of cooking. Traditional Indian clothing is known for its colorful and intricate designs, with women wearing sarees or salwar kameez and men wearing kurtas or dhotis.

In terms of art, India has a rich history of traditional art forms, including dance, music, painting, and sculpture. Some of the most famous Indian art forms include Bharatanatyam, Kathak, Kuchipudi, and Mohiniyattam. Indian architecture is also notable for its intricate carvings, domes, and minarets, with many famous monuments and buildings dotting the country's landscape.

In conclusion, India's cultural diversity is a source of pride for the country and its people. It is what makes India unique and fascinating to visitors from all over the world. Exploring India's diverse cultures and traditions is a journey of discovery that promises to be both educational and enlightening.

TWO

FESTIVALS AND CELEBRATIONS

India is a country that loves to celebrate, and its people have a rich tradition of festivals and celebrations. With so many different religions and cultural practices, there are a vast number of festivals celebrated across the country throughout the year.

Some of the major festivals celebrated in India include Diwali, Holi, Dussehra, Eid, Christmas, and many more. Each festival has its own unique significance, and the celebrations are usually filled with music, dance, feasting, and traditional activities.

Diwali, also known as the "Festival of Lights," is one of the most widely celebrated festivals in India. It is a Hindu festival that commemorates the victory of good over evil and light over darkness. People light up their homes and streets with diyas (earthen lamps), exchange sweets, and burst firecrackers to celebrate the occasion.

Holi, also known as the "Festival of Colors," is a Hindu festival that celebrates the arrival of spring. People play with colors and water, sing and dance, and enjoy delicious traditional sweets like gujiya and thandai.

Dussehra is another major Hindu festival that is celebrated all over India. It marks the victory of Lord Rama over the demon king Ravana and is celebrated with great fervor and enthusiasm. People burn effigies of Ravana, perform traditional dances like Dandiya and Garba, and exchange sweets and gifts.

Eid is a Muslim festival that marks the end of the month-long fast of Ramadan. People wear new clothes, visit each other, and enjoy traditional sweets like sevaiyaan.

Christmas is celebrated by Christians in India and is a joyous occasion for everyone. People decorate their homes, exchange gifts, and enjoy a traditional Christmas feast.

Apart from these major festivals, there are many other regional and local festivals that are unique to different parts of India. For example, the Ganesh Chaturthi festival is celebrated with great pomp and show in Maharashtra, while Onam is a major festival in Kerala.

In conclusion, festivals and celebrations are an integral part of India's rich cultural heritage. They bring people together, promote harmony, and provide an opportunity for individuals to express their religious and cultural beliefs. India is truly a land of festivals, and if you ever get a chance to visit the country, make sure to participate in one of the many celebrations that take place throughout the year.

THREE
RELIGION AND SPIRITUALITY

India is a land of diverse religions, beliefs, and practices, which play a significant role in shaping the country's culture and tradition. This chapter will provide an overview of some of the major religions and spiritual practices in India.

1. Hinduism: The largest religion in India, Hinduism is a complex and diverse religion that has evolved over thousands of years. It is characterized by a belief in multiple deities, with a particular focus on the god Vishnu, Shiva, and Brahma, and the goddesses Kali, Durga, and Lakshmi. Hinduism places great importance on karma, dharma, and reincarnation, and its followers believe in the cycle of birth, death, and rebirth. Rituals and festivals are a significant part of Hindu worship, with festivals such as Diwali, Holi, and Navratri being celebrated with great pomp and splendor across the country.

2. Buddhism: Buddhism is believed to have originated in India and spread to other parts of Asia. It is a non-theistic religion, which means that it does not believe in a personal God. Buddha, the founder of Buddhism, taught that the way to achieve enlightenment and liberation from the cycle of birth and rebirth is through the Eightfold Path. Buddhist teachings emphasize the importance of compassion, mindfulness, and non-attachment.

3. Islam: Islam is the second-largest religion in India and is believed to have been introduced to the country in the 7th century. It is a monotheistic religion, which means that its followers believe in one God, Allah. The pillars of Islam include the declaration of faith, prayer, charity, fasting, and the pilgrimage to Mecca. Muslims in India celebrate festivals such as Eid al-Fitr and Eid al-Adha with great enthusiasm.

4. Sikhism: Sikhism is a monotheistic religion founded in the 15th century by Guru Nanak. It emphasizes the importance of service to others, equality, and the oneness of God. Sikhism places great importance on the teachings of the ten Sikh gurus and the holy scripture, the Guru Granth Sahib. The religion's followers, known as Sikhs, celebrate the festival of Baisakhi, which marks the harvest season, and the birth anniversary of the founder of Sikhism, Guru Nanak.

5. Jainism: Jainism is an ancient religion that emphasizes the importance of non-violence, non-attachment, and self-discipline. Its followers believe in the existence of multiple deities, and the concept of karma, reincarnation, and liberation. Jainism places great importance on the five principles of non-violence, truth, non-stealing, celibacy, and non-attachment. Jains celebrate festivals such as Mahavir Jayanti, which marks the birth anniversary of Lord Mahavira, the last and most important Jain Tirthankara.

Conclusion: Religion and spirituality play a significant role in shaping the culture and tradition of India. The country's diverse religious practices, beliefs, and festivals offer a window into the rich spiritual heritage of this land. While this chapter provides only an overview of some of the major religions and practices, it offers a glimpse into the complex and multifaceted nature of India's spiritual traditions.

FOUR

Indian Cuisine

India is a country where food is not just about sustenance; it's an experience that tantalizes your taste buds and leaves you craving more. The cuisine of India is diverse, flavorful, and spicy, and is an integral part of the country's culture and tradition.

1. Regional Cuisine

India's vast landscape and diverse cultural heritage have resulted in a rich and varied cuisine that differs from region to region. From the tangy flavors of Maharashtra to the rich spices of Kerala, and the delicate aromas of the North East, each region has a unique culinary identity.

North Indian cuisine is famous for its rich curries, tandoori dishes, and bread. In contrast, South Indian cuisine is known for its extensive use of rice and coconut, and its delicate blend of spices. East Indian cuisine is characterized by its love for fish and seafood, while West Indian cuisine is a melting pot of flavors influenced by Gujarati, Maharashtrian, and Rajasthani cuisine.

2. Popular Dishes

No discussion on Indian cuisine is complete without mentioning some of its popular dishes. Some of the most well-known Indian dishes include:

* Butter Chicken: A creamy chicken curry cooked with butter, cream, and spices. It is a popular North Indian dish that is enjoyed with naan or rice.

* Biryani: A fragrant rice dish that is cooked with spices, vegetables, or meat, and sometimes fruits and nuts. It is a staple of South Indian cuisine and is enjoyed across the country.

* Masala Dosa: A crispy pancake made with a fermented batter of rice and lentils, stuffed with spiced potatoes, and served with coconut chutney and sambar. It is a popular breakfast dish in South India.

* Chole Bhature: A spicy chickpea curry that is served with deep-fried bread. It is a popular North Indian dish that is often enjoyed for breakfast or lunch.

3. Cooking Techniques

Indian cuisine is known for its intricate use of spices and cooking techniques. The use of a tawa (griddle) and tandoor (clay oven) is common in many dishes, and the masala (spice mix) is the heart of Indian cooking.

Spices are used extensively in Indian cooking, and each region has its unique blend of spices. Some of the commonly used spices include cumin, coriander, turmeric, cardamom, cinnamon, and cloves.

Vegetarianism is prevalent in India, and many popular dishes, such as chana masala and aloo gobi, are made with vegetables. Paneer (cottage cheese) is another ingredient that is popularly used in vegetarian dishes.

Conclusion

Indian cuisine is a reflection of the country's diverse cultural heritage and its love for food. It is an essential part of the country's culture and tradition, and it is enjoyed by people across the world. So, whether you are a fan of spicy food or just looking to try something new, the cuisine of India has something to offer everyone.

FIVE

ART AND CRAFT

India has a long and rich tradition of art and craft that reflects the country's diverse cultural heritage. The art and craft of India are as varied as the country's many regions, and each region has its unique artistic traditions. From the intricate paintings of Rajasthan to the colorful textiles of Gujarat, from the stunning wooden carvings of Kashmir to the exquisite pottery of Madhya Pradesh, India is a treasure trove of art and craft.

In this chapter, we'll explore some of the most famous art forms of India and their significance in Indian culture.

1. Paintings

Indian paintings are famous for their intricate details, bright colors, and unique style. Some of the most popular painting styles include:

* Madhubani painting: Originating in Bihar, this art form uses natural colors to depict deities, scenes from mythology, and social events.

* Rajasthani paintings: This style features vibrant colors, intricate details, and a focus on courtly life, hunting, and folk tales.

* Warli painting: Originating in Maharashtra, this art form uses simple geometric shapes and figures to depict scenes from daily life.

2. Textiles

India is famous for its textiles, which are renowned for their intricate designs and vivid colors. Some of the most famous textile styles include:

* Banarasi silk: Originating in Varanasi, this silk is known for its intricate weaving patterns and rich colors.

* Bandhani: Originating in Gujarat, this textile style involves the process of tie-dyeing to create intricate patterns and designs.

* Kalamkari: This style of hand-painted or block-printed textiles is famous for its intricate patterns and scenes from mythology.

3. Woodcarving

India is also famous for its woodcarving tradition, which has been passed down through generations. Some of the most famous woodcarvings include:

* Kashmiri woodcarvings: This style features intricate patterns and designs, often depicting scenes from nature, such as flowers and birds.

* South Indian woodcarvings: These carvings are famous for their intricate details and depictions of deities and mythological figures.

4. Pottery

India has a long tradition of pottery, and each region has its unique style. Some of the most famous pottery styles include:

* Blue pottery: Originating in Rajasthan, this pottery is known for its unique blue glaze and intricate designs.

* Terracotta pottery: This pottery style is popular in West Bengal and is known for its rustic charm and simplicity.

In addition to these art forms, India is also famous for its jewelry, sculptures, and metalwork.

Indian art and craft are deeply rooted in Indian culture and reflect the country's rich heritage. They are not just objects of beauty but also a means of passing on stories, myths, and cultural values from one generation to another. By exploring the art and craft of India, you'll gain a deeper understanding of Indian culture and its significance.

SIX

ARCHITECTURE AND MONUMENTS

India is home to some of the most awe-inspiring and magnificent architectural wonders in the world. The country's rich history and diverse cultural heritage have given rise to a unique blend of architectural styles that are unparalleled in their beauty and grandeur.

Indian architecture spans several millennia and is a testament to the country's artistic and cultural diversity. From the ancient Indus Valley civilization to the modern era, India's architecture has undergone several transformations, reflecting the evolution of its society and culture.

In this chapter, we will take a closer look at some of India's most famous architectural monuments and explore the history and significance of each.

1. Taj Mahal: One of the most iconic symbols of India, the Taj Mahal is a magnificent mausoleum located in the city of Agra. Built by the Mughal Emperor Shah Jahan in memory of his beloved wife, Mumtaz Mahal, the Taj Mahal is a stunning example of Mughal architecture. The monument is adorned with intricate carvings, calligraphy, and beautiful inlaid designs made of precious stones.

2. Red Fort: Located in the heart of Old Delhi, the Red Fort is a historic monument that was built by Mughal Emperor Shah Jahan.

The fort was the seat of power of the Mughal empire for nearly two centuries and is an excellent example of Mughal architecture. The fort is famous for its stunning red sandstone walls and its beautiful gardens.

3. Hawa Mahal: The Hawa Mahal, or the Palace of the Winds, is a five-story palace located in the heart of Jaipur. Built in 1799, the palace is a stunning example of Rajput architecture and is famous for its intricate latticework and the hundreds of small windows that allow for the free flow of air, hence the name "Palace of the Winds."

4. Khajuraho Temple: The Khajuraho temple complex is a group of ancient Hindu and Jain temples located in Madhya Pradesh. Built between the 9th and 10th centuries, the temples are famous for their stunningly intricate carvings, depicting a range of subjects, including gods and goddesses, mythical creatures, and erotic scenes.

5. Qutub Minar: The Qutub Minar is a towering minaret located in Delhi and is one of the most recognizable landmarks of the city. Built by Qutub-ud-din Aibak, the first Muslim ruler of Delhi, the minaret is an excellent example of Indo-Islamic architecture and is adorned with beautiful carvings and intricate calligraphy.

India's architecture is a treasure trove of history and culture. The monuments and buildings are a testament to the country's rich and diverse past, and they continue to inspire awe and wonder in visitors from around the world. A visit to these architectural wonders is a must for anyone interested in exploring India's culture and tradition.

SEVEN

DAILY LIFE AND SOCIETY

India's society is deeply rooted in tradition and customs, and the daily life of its people reflects this. The country's culture places great emphasis on family, community, and hospitality, and these values are integral to Indian society.

1. Family Life: Family is at the heart of Indian society. The concept of the joint family, where multiple generations live together, is still prevalent in many parts of the country. Elders are respected and revered, and their opinions are highly valued. In many households, family members share meals, and it's common for them to gather together for festivals and celebrations.

2. Social Norms: India is a conservative society, and certain social norms and customs are strictly followed. Dressing modestly is highly valued, and public displays of affection are not common. Respect for elders and authority is an integral part of Indian society, and addressing others with respect and using proper titles is highly valued.

3. Gender Roles: In India, gender roles are often deeply ingrained in society, and there are certain expectations for men and women. While women have made significant strides in many aspects of society, they are still often expected to prioritize their family responsibilities over their careers.

4. Hospitality: Hospitality is an essential aspect of Indian culture. Guests are treated with great respect and are often given a warm welcome. It's common for people to offer food and drinks to their guests, and the hosts often go out of their way to make their guests feel comfortable.

5. Daily Life: Daily life in India varies depending on the region and the individual's socioeconomic status. Many people still work in agriculture, and the rhythm of life is often dictated by the seasons. Urban areas have a fast-paced lifestyle, with many people working in the service sector. It's common for people to commute long distances to work, and traffic congestion is a common problem.

Conclusion: The daily life and society of India are unique and reflect the country's cultural heritage. The importance of family, community, and hospitality are integral to Indian society, and these values have been passed down from generation to generation. Despite the challenges of modernization and globalization, these values remain at the heart of Indian culture and continue to shape the daily lives of its people.

Epilogue

As we come to the end of our journey exploring India's culture and tradition, it's hard not to feel overwhelmed by the sheer depth and richness of this country's heritage. We've traveled through time, from ancient Vedic times to the present day, and we've witnessed the evolution of a civilization that has embraced diversity, spirituality, and community in all aspects of life.

One of the key takeaways from this exploration is the importance of community and family in Indian society. India has always placed a high value on relationships, and family and community bonds are at the heart of this society. We've seen this reflected in the way people come together to celebrate festivals and in the way people take care of their elders and extended families.

Another key aspect of Indian culture is its spirituality. Religion plays an important role in everyday life in India, and we've explored the different beliefs and practices of major religions such as Hinduism, Islam, Sikhism, and Christianity. The reverence for nature, the importance of meditation and yoga, and the belief in karma are some of the spiritual values that permeate Indian society.

We've also explored India's diverse cuisine, art, and architecture, each of which is a reflection of the country's cultural and regional diversity. The delicious cuisine, vibrant art forms, and awe-inspiring architecture are a testament to the creativity and skill of the people of India.

Finally, we've seen how India has embraced modernity while holding onto its cultural roots. As we've explored India's daily life and society, we've seen how traditional values and customs coexist with the modern way of life. It's this unique blend of tradition and modernity that makes India such a fascinating and dynamic country.

In conclusion, we hope this journey has been an enriching experience for you, and that you've gained a deeper appreciation for India's culture and tradition. We encourage you to continue exploring this fascinating country and its heritage, and to immerse yourself in the vibrant and colorful tapestry of India's past and present. Thank you for joining us on this incredible journey!

www.ingramcontent.com/pod-product-compliance
Lightning Source LLC
Chambersburg PA
CBHW020946160726
47993CB00007B/2966